Real Estate Investment : No Longer a Dream

Aditi Chopra

ACKNOWLEDGEMENT

I want to acknowledge my husband, Vimal Chopra for his guidance and help in writing this book.

Preface

The day it all began, at least in my mind was when I was attending a leadership training a few years ago. One of my colleagues asked me a question out of the blue, "What would you do if I gave you a million dollars?"

I didn't have to think a lot before I replied, "I would buy a beach house!"

I came home that day and narrated the incident to my husband. Later I started thinking, do I really need to win a lottery or wait for someone to give me loads of money? Can I not look for my dream vacation home now?

That's how it all started and we have gone through an adventurous journey since then. We have done a lot of research and learned a lot from our experiences. We have invested in single family homes as well as vacation homes. As part of this process, we have gained experience in analyzing various property types and getting the right type of mortgage. We have also learned how best to advertise a property and come up with the right pricing model in order to maximize cash flow.

We have helped and coached quite a few of our friends on how to enter the real estate market and have given a jump-start to some of them with their own investments. I would like to make all of these real life experiences available to my readers in this book.

This beginner's guide is a view into the opportune world of real estate investment. It is also designed to help fulfill dreams of anyone who has a dream similar to mine.

I know that before stepping into the real estate market, an investor has a lot of questions on his mind. He is excited as well as nervous about entering the market. Nothing can soothe those nerves better than hearing in detail the real life experiences of those who have ventured into the market before them. Most people have experience in buying their own home but do not have any experience with rental properties. Your approach and research that worked for your home purchase may not work when choosing a rental property.

There are a number of books on real estate investment. You can also attend seminars on the subject. However, a lot of the material in these books is theoretical and written from a real estate professional's perspective. A number of these books focus on "how to get rich quick". In most cases, there is no way to get rich quickly but instead one should follow a steady model in order to gain in the long term. My goal in this book is to share our experience, both good and bad, so that you are armed with practical information when you venture into your own investments.

Since this book is written from personal experiences, it offers a unique perspective for a first time investor keeping in mind the most frequently asked questions. In addition to answering those queries, this book also addresses all the concerns of a beginner. The many practical scenarios mentioned in this book will help first time investors in their journey and give them the confidence to venture into the real estate investment industry.

Aditi Chopra

CONTENTS

1 WHY INVEST IN REAL ESTATE?

With all the different investment choices available to an investor today, why would one choose real estate? Why not take the easier route of investing in mutual funds? If I were writing this book in the 1990s, I would have said why not invest in stocks? We have seen how the stock market has performed in the last few years and why stocks and even mutual funds are no longer a safe investment. Real estate has not been immune to the recent downturn and we have seen the once "safe" real estate market taken a downturn in different parts of the United States. Foreclosures and short sales have littered the market along with mortgages that were written with no down payments which also contributed greatly to the recent economic downturn. Considering how the mortgage industry and real estate have performed in the last few years, one may question whether real estate investment is a safe choice?

The answer to the above question is not that straightforward. We don't know, neither can we predict, if real estate has hit rock bottom. However, we do know that some properties are much better priced from a buyer's perspective than they were five years ago. We don't know for sure what their upward price potential is but being at such low prices, upward potential is more probable than not. The goal is not to just buy real estate for appreciation, since we do not know when the market will turn around. If you buy smartly, take a reasonable amount of loan and are able to pay for the property by renting it out, over a long period of time you will make money. I am not preaching buying houses cheaply and flipping them for a huge profit overnight. I believe that mentality is what got the housing market into trouble.

Internet has revolutionized pretty much every industry. Information is easily available and sometimes we even have an overload of information. One industry where it has probably made the biggest difference is real estate.

I remember pre-internet days when we had pretty much no access to real estate data. We would have to solely rely on the real estate agents. When my husband and I bought our first house in the pre-internet days, our agent would run the comps, print it out, and fax it to us. If we wanted to look at a house with different criteria or in a different neighborhood we needed to go through the process all over again. Furthermore if a buyer would like to do some pre-analysis to better utilize both their own and their agent's time effectively they could not do so. This is not the case today. There is plenty of information available for anyone who wants to enter the real estate market. This access to data and information on properties helps both the investor and the real estate agent. Decisions are made faster and better. There are no regrets on either end and today's investor is more happy and satisfied. This is another reason real estate investment is feasible and a more practical and safer choice than few years ago. A good real estate agent is still a critical piece of your team though.

A comprehensive website to start with is http://www.zillow.com/. Anyone can figure out the expected value of a house, compare it with other properties, and look for the history of a property. Zillow is a comprehensive website for today's investor, providing FAQs and the latest information on mortgages, rental properties and homes. Zillow also provides summary information in the general area and price trends. You should use this information as a starting point since individual homes may vary in price depending upon the upgrades or lack there of.

Mortgage rates are quite low, in fact perhaps near an all time low. This makes real estate investment even more attractive since the carrying cost of the property becomes lower. Many people have had to foreclose their home and have had a dent in their credit history. It is hard for them to get new loans due to more strict rules around loan applications. These people are used to living in single family homes and therefore have increased the rental pool. Low mortgage rates and a stable rental market ensures that rental income will be stable as well for the real estate investor.

A typical investor is advised to diversify his portfolio. The saying goes, "Don't put all your eggs in one basket". Therefore, even if you have invested in stocks, bonds or mutual funds, keeping all your funds invested in a risky portfolio is not a wise choice. Real estate returns are perhaps not as high as potentially those of stocks but they are real and less risky. Balancing your portfolio between risky and not so risky investment is a wise choice.

From a more personal perspective, all of the above reasons provided us an incentive to enter the real estate market as well. The biggest advantage was the availability of information from the internet resources. If it were not for that, we would have probably hesitated or taken a longer time in making the move into this lucrative market.

Advantages of Real Estate Investment

Besides being less risky and a more feasible investment choice, real estate investment has long term benefits as well. One obvious benefit is the cash flow that you receive on an ongoing basis from your rental income. In addition, if you choose your property carefully, there is a potential value increase in the future. It is similar to getting a dividend on your stock in addition to an increased stock price. Real estate investment is also a good option for your retirement age. If you plan well in advance, your rental income will keep providing a steady stream of income when you retire. Wouldn't it be nice to not have to worry about a steady income when you retire from work so you can relax and focus on your hobbies instead? You could also use real estate investments for your childrens' education, especially if they are still young. You can rent out the property, keep the cash flow and later sell it in order to fund your childrens' education when they are ready to go to college.

In order to fully comprehend this scenario, you would have to think long term and not in the present. To put it a bit differently, when you invest in a real estate property, your renters are paying for it and over time you will fully own the property with no mortgage. You can even hand down these properties to your children. You have to become a visionary for your life and then execute that golden vision. Real estate investments provide fruits of your labor in the long run so if you are about ten to fifteen years from retirement age, then is the best time to think about real estate investments.

There are tax advantages of owning real estate investment properties, and I cover them in more details later in this book. In summary, unlike a stock dividend or the interest you receive from the bank (which is fully taxable in the year you receive it), real estate income generally gets offset by "depreciation" you take on the property. Furthermore, if in the future you sell the property, you can do a "like-exchange" and in theory maintain the original cost basis of your property forever. Wouldn't it be nice if such an option was available when you buy and sell stocks?

Things to watch out for

You might be thinking, well all this is great but what is the downside associated with real estate investment? And why is everyone not jumping into it? Well, for one, investing in real estate is not easy. It requires discipline and work. If you are used to trading stocks and mutual funds while comfortably sitting in your chair, you are in for a surprise with real estate investment. It is not as simple as a few mouse clicks. It is also not as simple as researching on your favorite real estate website. It requires more work than that. Even after you have acquired a property, there is work involved in renting and managing it. Of course you could outsource most of the work but in that case, it will cut into your cash flow. You need to run your real estate investments as any other business. Although unlike other businesses even if you do most of work yourself, you can do it in your free time and it takes much less effort. Some of this work has become easier with internet but I want to say upfront, real estate investing is not going to be a cake walk.

Real estate property can and sometimes does lose value over a period of time. Even though you are cash flow positive on a monthly basis, you may realize that you overpaid for your property. This possibility is why it is important to take your time, do your research thoroughly and purchase a property judiciously. Look at the area, choose your property wisely, buy it at the right price and rent it while minimizing your costs.

2 YOUR GOAL, OPTIONS, AND PROCESS

If you are reading this chapter, you may already be convinced that real estate investment is a good choice for you. You are all buckled up to do what it takes to be an investor. If so, your next question would be where do I start? What are the different real estate investment choices available for me? Which one of those choices will suit my lifestyle? The answer really lies in your investment goal with real estate. It is very important to first identify your goal.

When my husband and I were starting off, we had pretty much the same questions and concerns in mind. Our starting point was the internet due to the wide range of resources available on the web. I would urge you to start your research there. For example, if you are looking at a potential property, utilize the internet resources to checkout the schools in the area, the economic and demographic layout, and all the variables that come to mind.

What is your goal?

In order to identify your goal, you need to realize that there are a number of options when you invest in real estate. It really depends on how much time and money you can invest in the project. You could start small with a townhouse or a single family home depending on your budget. The advantage with this option is the simplicity associated with it. This is the option to choose for an investor whose goal is pure investment.

Rule of Thumb : For pure investment purposes, the number one rule to consider is that you always want to be cash flow positive. What that means is if you can subtract all your expenses related with real estate property from the rental income on a monthly basis, you should be ahead of the game. You don't ever want your expenses to exceed the rental income. If that is the case, you probably didn't do your homework right. If you are cash flow negative over time, you will probably start wondering why you invested in real estate.

You could also look at vacation homes. An investor who wants to enjoy the vacation home and at the same time rent it to offset some of the costs of owning a vacation home should look at this option.

Besides looking at the budget, you need to also understand the amount of work and maintenance involved in each of these options. Some people start with acquiring a timeshare property to avoid having to do any work but I don't recommend timeshare as a good investment option since it can be limiting. Timeshares are always a money loser. If you calculate the weekly cost times the number of weeks in a year, you will soon realize that the total is almost three to four times the cost of the actual property. Furthermore look closely at the annual fees you pay.

Typically it will be four to five times the expense of a comparable furnished vacation home.

Some investors are looking at real estate purely as an income and would not want to mix income with the pleasure of a vacation home. You as an investor have to first determine what your motivations are. This will help you narrow down your choices and work towards a concrete goal.

Another option to look at is international properties. The work involved is obviously much more in the case of international property but it does have an added advantage of lower buying price as compared to an equivalent property in the United States. An investor who is adventurous could find this option quite lucrative and may want to venture into the unknown of foreign investment. This is a very different option when compared to single family homes and vacation home. I will discuss this topic more in a later chapter.

Purchase price is important

In order to gain in real estate investment, purchasing at the right price is extremely important no matter which investment option you go with. In more expensive areas, such as coastal areas, the property price is significantly higher, and the rent you can charge will probably not cover the cost. Hence you will not be able to have a positive cash flow. When investors buy property in such an area they are counting on "appreciation" which may or may not be there. The last thing you want is an investment into which you have to keep putting your own money on a monthly basis. This will take a toll on you sooner than later.

If you go to a real estate agent or attend a seminar, you want to be able to have an intelligent discussion with them on the topic of positive cash flow. This is especially true if you are looking at vacation homes where it is much harder to anticipate whether you will be cash flow positive or not. For rental income and frequency, you will have to look at statistical data and extrapolate. You need to be able to ask this data from your real estate agent and not jump the gun on purchasing a property and end up with a cash flow negative situation.

How to calculate Cash Flow

Monthly Rental Income

less mortgage payment (Principal + Interest)

less property tax

less other expenses (HOA, home insurance etc.)

= Cash Flow

Your real estate team

You are now convinced that you want to enter the real estate investment market and you are wondering what the process is and how to execute it.

You obviously need to research the area in which you want to purchase property. Everything else being the same, the best place to invest is closer to where you live. This way you can keep a closer look at your properties and act as your own property manager (if you have time and the passion to do so). In a lot of cases this may not be feasible due to higher property cost and lower rents for comparable properties. For example, if you live in California it is typically not possible to find properties that you can rent out and break even on cash flow on a monthly basis. If this is the case you should venture out of your area to look for other opportunities. The process itself is not that complicated but you certainly need to assemble a good trustworthy team to support you in carrying out your vision.

Real estate agent - Once you have identified the area where you want to invest, you need to find a reliable real estate agent who specializes in investment properties. He should be able to run the numbers for you as well as do the required research to advise you on the merits of a property. Finding an agent you trust and feel comfortable with may not be an easy task, but it is extremely important to do so before you go too far into your venture. If you are doing long distance investments, it is even more important since you will rely on the agent to look at the property and give you advice. A typical real estate agent may not think like an investor so having that expertise is necessary. They should be able to run both the sales comparisons and rental comps in your area of interest. Remember, knowing what you can expect to rent a property for is as important as having the sales comps when you are trying to calculate cash flow and evaluate whether the property is a good investment.

Mortgage broker - You need a good mortgage broker who specializes in investment properties and can get you a reasonable loan and close in a short time. These days, banks often take a long time to close on loans so expediency is an important consideration. There are additional rules for investment properties and I will discuss in a later chapter how they differ from your primary mortgage.

Home inspector – You need to find a good home inspector who will inspect the property you are considering thoroughly. The inspection will allow you to know what needs to be fixed and approximately how much it will cost before you decide to acquire the property. Your real estate agent may be able to identify a reputable inspector for you. Ask potential inspectors if you can see a sample report that they have done for another property so you can evaluate the depth of their expertise. They should have lots of photos of the property, especially of areas where they find any deficiencies.

Property manager – A property manager helps you find tenants and takes care of your property. This is especially important if you are investing outside of the area where you live and you will be interacting with them the most during the rental process. You need to find someone who will take care of your property as their own. Sometimes it is better to go with a "property manager" who is an individual rather than a bigger company. This way you will have only one person to interact with rather than a team of people. It is easier to build trust and understanding with one individual as opposed to a team of people.

CPA – A CPA may be able to help you with taxation and other aspects of owning a rental property.

You as an investor – You are the most critical member of this team. Remember no one takes care of your finances better than you. All the other professionals in your team only get paid when you buy the property. You need to have enough information and be educated in various aspects so that you can ask them the right questions and evaluate their advice. You cannot know all the aspects of real estate investments when you buy the first property (although you will understand investing and become more educated as you move along) and this is why it is critical to do your best to identify the right professionals for your team. Any member of your team who pressures you into making decisions may not be the right fit. Of course they should be able to provide an opinion to steer you into the right direction and that is definitely a plus. Treat all members of your team with respect and follow through in a timely manner. You need to demonstrate to your team member that you are a serious investor and value their time and advice. The professional gets paid only when you make the transaction so use their time wisely. If you are just kicking tires, don't engage them too much. Just mention that you will reach out to them when you are ready.

From the renter's perspective

At this point, I want to emphasize the importance of looking at a real estate investment property from the renter's perspective. If you are a home owner, forget everything you like in that home and why you picked it. When you are in the market hunting for an investment property that you are going to be renting out, you need to get in the mind of a renter. What would they like, what would they care about? If they were shopping for a rental, what kind of competitive analysis would they do and how can you make your property rise above the competition.

This approach may sound obvious but to be able to translate it into practice is easier said than done. When you buy a home for yourself you may be looking for upgraded floors, a granite kitchen, large square footage, etc.. Someone looking for a rental property does not necessarily care for lots of upgrades. More important is the layout of the house, size and functional aspects, schools etc. It is eye-opening to profile a typical good renter for each type of property. For single family homes the emphasis is on proximity to schools, jobs, and amenities in the community. Typically a single family home in a master planned community with good schools provides for a good rental pool. Upgrades in a single family home may help you to get the place rented sooner but may not provide for extra rent. A renter may like to have those expensive upgrades but would they pay more rent for it? An extra $100 in the rent may take you out of a wider rental pool.

For vacation homes, renters' preference will depend on places that they would like to visit. Renters of all sorts are very price conscious. If you have a vacation home, on lets say the 30th floor of a high rise building, can you demand a higher rent for it? Probably not, and therefore when you are buying your property, you don't want to overpay to purchase a vacation home on 30th floor. It might lead to a cash flow negative situation. At the same time if you want to splurge a little because you feel like staying on the 30th floor or you are getting a good value on the property, then go for it.

If you have an international vacation home, is that country frequently visited by travelers? Is there something unique or attractive about that country that can attract vacationers? Even if the country you have in mind is not so popular as a destination today, does it have the potential to become one? Have other big names like Donald Trump invested in real estate in this country. If not, why not?

It is very important to get inside the renter's mind and think from that perspective before making your decision. Today's renter is very savvy, and he has all the resources on the internet to do his research before making up his mind.

Bottom-line, you make money in real estate primarily if you acquire the property at a good price. Over a long period of time your renters pay down the mortgage on the property and in the future you own it free and clear.

3 SINGLE FAMILY HOMES

As discussed in chapter two, single family homes are one of the most viable options for the first time investor. They tend to maintain their pricing better over other types of properties. When you plan to sell a single family home, your pool of potential buyers includes both investors and people looking to buy a home for their own family.

Both the buying and selling of a single family home is a safer and easier process than some of the other investment options, especially for those who already own a home. If the single family homes in your area are expensive, you could consider a more affordable option of purchasing a townhome. The disadvantage of owning a townhome is that it comes with a monthly HOA (home owner association) payment that you need to consider when doing your cash flow calculation. Also, townhomes tend to appreciate less than a comparable single family home. Remember, the number one rule is to be cash flow positive when you get into the real estate investment business. Renters prefer a single family home to townhomes but if the townhomes are roomy and spacious, they are a good sell to the renters as well. Location is a consideration also. For example, a townhome in California may be a good choice while in Texas it may not be desirable. Land is plentiful in Texas and people typically prefer a single family home over a townhome.

What to look for when purchasing single family home?

Many factors need to be considered before you purchase a single family home or townhouse for investment purposes. There is a terminology used in real estate - location, location, location. While location is an extremely important aspect to consider, you also need to factor in the purchase cost and the projected cash flow before acquiring rental properties.

The first thing to consider, of course, is the price of the property. You must determine whether the rental income in the area will be enough for you as an investor to be cash flow positive. Don't buy a property unless you are sure about being cash flow positive. The last thing you want to do is pay the mortgage from your own pocket month after month.

Typically a three or four bedroom house is a good choice. If this is an older neighborhood, chances are the typical size is three bedroom. But if you can find a four bedroom (approx 2000 – 2400 square foot home) it will appeal to a broader set of families. i.e. a family with two children.

Do not buy a very big home since you may limit your pool of potential renters. A larger home is more expensive and you need a higher rent to produce cash flow, and typically renters do not want a very big home. The same logic applies to homes in the best school district. The higher price that you will pay to acquire such a property may be not be compensated by the slightly higher rent that you can command. You should run the cash flow numbers to determine this.

You also need to look at the neighborhood. Is it safe, is it a growing market in terms of job and economy and companies? Would renters prefer staying in this area versus other areas of the city? Are the schools of this neighborhood good enough? The answers to these questions will be of interest to a family considering renting the property. Are groceries stores and malls accessible from the rental property? Normally that should not be an issue but sometimes, in newer construction areas, the lack of nearby shopping could be a problem.

Buying a home in a good school district is important, but buying one in the best school district where home prices are much higher may not provide enough higher rent to produce good cash flow. Look for a balance between cash flow potential and a good school district.

Another aspect to look at is whether in the neighborhood most people are home owners or renters. There could be several reasons why a certain neighborhood appeals more to home owners, instead of renters and you need to be aware of that. You don't want to be struggling to find renters for your property.

If you are a hands-on person in terms of fixing and enhancing a home, you could also look at the option of finding a good deal on a not so well maintained single family home and then do the work on it on an economical scale. This way your cost basis is well under the mark and you are much more cash flow positive. My husband and I didn't venture into this area since we were not so keen on doing the work to enhance a property but this is a very lucrative option for a number of investors.

On a personal note, my husband and I attended some seminars on real estate in order to complement our own research. The information we gained there was beneficial when we were looking at single family homes in areas we were not familiar with. We could ask area related questions during these seminars and get more insight into the trends and intricacies of that particular region. For example, in some states, having the master bedroom downstairs in a two story house was the norm. But in other states, having the master bedroom downstairs was out of the norm. When you are purchasing your rental property, you need to also look at these factors so you don't purchase something that is the "odd one out".

One thing my husband and I learned was that in order to remain cash flow positive, our purchase prices needed to be as low as possible. We were living in a state where house prices were typically high and therefore investing in homes for rental in that state would not have been a sound decision. After doing some research and visiting a few states where real estate was typically more affordable, we narrowed our field down to a few states where we could purchase good properties on a reasonable cost basis. Georgia and Texas seemed to be good choice for a typical first time investor to purchase single family homes. We focused on newer properties in master planned communities with good school district to attract a good profile of renters.

How to determine offer price on a property?

You worked with your real estate agent that identified a property that you like and are ready to make an offer. The big question is how much should you offer? Your real estate agent should provide you with comparable sale prices in the immediate neighborhood. Typically they will only include properties that are similar (i.e about same number of rooms and similar square footage that have sold in the last three months). This is a good way to determine comparable sales but I recommend that you ask them for additional comparable data. For example, ask them to include all homes (large or small) in the neighborhood and ask them for sales data for the last two years. You want to compare the subject property to a wider set of criteria than is typically used. Once you determine the fair price of the property, you can test by offering a slightly lower price. I don't suggest you to offer 15 to 20 percent lower than the asking price but it does not hurt to offer say 5 percent below the fair market value. Remember that you are buying this property as an investment and not for personal use. If you don't succeed in reaching a deal after a couple of times then you will know the true value of properties in the neighborhood. Your real estate agent should be understanding if he realizes that you are trying to get the best price but are still sincere in your offer and commitment to buy a property. Remember your agent gets paid only when you buy a property so you have to balance their time and effort as well. Also, when making an offer you can agree to other terms such as a fast closing to make your offer more attractive to the seller.

Example of cash flow calculation

While evaluating properties we realized the 1 percent rule. Basically if you can rent a property for 1 percent or more of the purchase price of the property, you will be cash flow positive.

Lets take an example of a typical property with a purchase price of $140k. Lets assume you put a 20 percent down payment and take a 15 year fixed loan on $112k at 4 percent (please note that the interest rate for rental properties is slightly higher than for personal properties). Let's assume you will pay a monthly HOA fees of $25 and manage the property yourself. Going by the above mentioned 1 percent rule, let's further assume that you are getting a rental income of $1400 per month on this property. Your cash flow calculation will be as follows:

Monthly Rental income = $1400
Monthly Mortgage payment = $828 (Principal + Interest)
Monthly HOA fees = $25
Monthly property tax = $145
Monthly insurance expense = $75

Monthly Cash Flow = $1400 - $828 - $25 - $145 - $75 = $327

This example translates to a yearly cash flow of $3924 assuming the property is rented throughout the year. The key is to always be cash flow positive. In this case, the investor is in the safe positive cash flow zone. If the investor can get a higher rent, his cash flow will rise but for the purposes of calculation, I would advise you to use less aggressive numbers.

Lets do the same calculation with a 30 year fixed mortgage.

Monthly Rental income = $1400
Monthly Mortgage payment = $534 (Principal + Interest)
Monthly HOA fees = $25
Monthly property tax = $145
Monthly insurance expense = $75

Monthly Cash Flow = $1400 - $534 - $25 - $145 - $75 = $621

The numbers look much better on a 30 year fixed loan.

Of course I have not accounted for property management fees and any vacancies that may vary depending on your situation. At worst you are cash flow even. After fifteen years or thirty years, depending on your loan, you no longer have a mortgage and you own the property free and clear. Your property may or may not appreciate during this time.

The other thing to note is that a big chunk of your mortgage payment is going towards the principal of your loan. You need to understand this key real estate investments fact that you are paying down your principal and over time your property will be all paid off.

Your cost is mostly fixed during the life of the loan since it is a fixed loan. The rental rate may increase in the future due to inflation and should help improve the cash flow. If you fast forward five years, your payments are still almost the same although now a bigger portion of your mortgage payment is going towards principal. In the above example, most probably your rental income can increase in the future to $1550 or more, hence helping increase the cash flow.

4 VACATION HOMES

Lets move towards the slightly more involved option of investing in a vacation home. Besides it being an involved option and somewhat more complicated than investing in a single family home, the motivation to invest in a vacation home is also different. For an investor who is not only looking at real estate as an investment but also wants to enjoy and own a vacation home, this is the choice to go after. Buy a vacation home only if you would like to enjoy the property yourself. Vacation homes can provide extra income to offset the cost of ownership but if you would never visit the place yourself, probably you should consider a more traditional rental property with longer term renters.

With a vacation home, you get to enjoy it on your vacations as well as make some rental income on it when you are not using it yourself. The drawback however is that it is a lot more work to rent out a vacation home as compared to a single family home. You as an investor have to make the choice based on your motivation and desires.

Your vacation home is in competition with hotels and other vacation homes in the same area and therefore it also requires more work to stay above the competition. Competition also exists for single family homes and town homes but the scale here is much bigger. There are more hotel rooms and condominiums for rental than let's say single family homes. Renter's choice in case of vacation home can vary quite a bit.

Renting a vacation home is not a necessity, it is a luxury unlike renting a single family home on a daily basis. Renters have different preference on vacation homes and usually prefer to have a view or easy access to the beach or casino or pool or spa and other amenities. You need to be able to keep all of these factors in mind when deciding on what kind of vacation home you are aiming for.

I believe your number one consideration is your own choice of vacation home but you also need to be able to rent it out to cover your cost and stay cash flow positive.

What to look for when purchasing a vacation home

There are many factors to consider before purchasing a vacation rental property. First, it needs to be a place you would like to visit often. Primarily it is your vacation home and secondarily you are going to be renting it to make additional income. If you like to ski, you may want to look for a place where it snows in winter and has reasonable activities to do in summer as well. If you are a beach kind of person, you would want to purchase a vacation home on a beach. If Las Vegas is your game, then a Las Vegas condominium is the way to go. You need to choose a favorite place where you would not become bored if you went there every year or even multiple times in a year.

The other factor to keep in mind is the cash flow projection. Do your careful analysis before purchasing a vacation rental property. Consider all the maintenance costs that come with owning a vacation home and then look at a typical rental amount in the area for condominiums or hotels. This information is necessary so you don't go cash flow negative. Vacation homes require an additional insurance because you are renting it to many renters as opposed to long term leases. This means your insurance cost will be higher for a vacation home as compared to a single family home. Sometimes taking a studio versus a one bedroom condominium has a make or break effect on the cash flow potential because HOA fees are larger for a one bedroom condominium. Be aware of all costs before making your decision. Ask for all the empirical data for rentals from previous years, and do your own research as well.

When you look at the rental data for a vacation home, be mindful of which year the data covers and how the economic conditions were during that year. Real estate professionals could have sliced and diced the data to make it look more lucrative than it really is. Look behind the picture, not only the way it is painted to you. Economic conditions can vary the data one way or the other. I would also recommend you use less aggressive numbers when doing your cash flow analysis. This way you avoid any kind of future disappointment. Furthermore unlike single family homes that are on annual lease, the occupancy rate on a vacation rental may be lower. In high seasons you may be close to 100 percent booked whereas in low seasons it may be much lower occupancy rates. A good measure is to determine hotel occupancy rates in the area. You can also check other vacation rentals that are currently in the market and how booked they are into the calendar. You can check this using vrbo.com and other vacation rental websites. You should also look at what other owners are asking as rental rates for properties in similar areas.

Example of cash flow calculation

Let's look at a typical vacation home property with a purchase price of $170,000. Let's assume, the investor pays 20 percent down payment. The loan is going to be for $136,000. Let's assume the loan is 15 year fixed with a mortgage rate of 4 percent (please note that interest rate for rental properties is slightly higher than personal properties)

Lets say the vacation home is in a touristy place and the investor is able to keep it rented throughout the year. On average his daily rental income is $90. Monthly HOA fees will include the insurance payment of the vacation rental. Lets assume that the investor is not using a property manager and is managing the rental himself. The cash flow calculation will look as follows:

Monthly Rental income = $2700
Monthly Mortgage payment = $1006 (Principal + Interest)
Monthly property tax = $177
Monthly HOA fee = $600

Cash Flow = $2700 - $1006 - $177 - $600 = $917

In the above example, the investor is safely cash flow positive. This may not be the case if he used the vacation home primarily for his personal usage or was not able to rent it out enough to cover expenses. However if we calculate on a yearly basis, he should be cash flow positive or cash flow even at least. Even if he was slightly cash flow negative, it shouldn't be a lot. Remember, in this case the goal of the investor is not pure business but to own a vacation home. In addition to having a vacation home, he is covering the expenses by renting it out while not using it himself. Typically vacation homes have high maintenance costs associated with them, so be fully aware of these costs before making a purchase.

Looking at the above example you may think that this cash flow looks better as compared to the single family home example. In that case, why should I invest in single family home at all? What you need to keep in mind is that for vacation rental, the occupancy rate may fluctuate. It requires more work on an ongoing basis to keep it fully rented. Occupancy rate also gets affected by other factors such as people cutting down on travel expenditure in an economic downturn. Single family homes are safer since they are less affected by these fluctuations.

If I did the cash flow calculation for 70 percent occupancy rate in the above example, it would look as follows :

Monthly Rental income = $1890
Monthly Mortgage payment = $1006 (Principal + Interest)
Monthly property tax = $177
Monthly HOA fee = $600

Cash Flow $= \$1890 - \$1006 - \$177 - \$600 = \$107$

As you can see, with 70 percent occupancy rate, the investor is not so much cash flow positive. Again, his motivation for owning a vacation home was different. It was for both personal usage as well as supplemental income. I don't believe we can compare cash flow calculation of a single family home with that of a vacation home since the goal in both cases is different. What is common in both cases is that the investor must do his cash flow calculation ahead of time before making the purchase.

Regulations on vacation homes

Some cities and communities have restrictions on an owner's ability to rent out property for short term rentals. Short term is typically defined anything less than six months. It is very important for you to find out if your prospective vacation home has any such restrictions. Furthermore if you are renting the property on a weekly or short term basis you need to have a business license and collect occupancy tax from the renters. Since the rules of each area are different, it is very important to become familiar with them before you buy a vacation home.

5 INTERNATIONAL VACATION HOMES

If you are feeling brave, you can also look at investing in an international property. Again this would be for an investor who is not looking at the purchase purely from an investment point of view but is treating this property as a vacation home. An investor who loves traveling and is more adventurous in exploring different countries of the world may find this option quite lucrative.

There are several advantages of looking for an international vacation home, including more affordable pricing. Typically a beach house in the United States will be far more expensive than a beach house in Mexico. Personally, I like the excitement that comes with unknown. With international vacation homes, you are getting into some unknown territories. This is certainly exciting but also a lot of work because now you have to work with international laws or rather laws of the foreign country, their banking system, how they handle real estate and other considerations.

In addition to saving on the investment dollars by purchasing a more affordable vacation home in another country, if you do your research, you may gain other benefits such as saving on property tax. Some countries waive property taxes for a number of years to attract foreign investment.

You could purchase a luxurious ocean front property for an affordable price. Some countries such as Dubai do not allow foreign investors to own real estate but there are other countries that provide incentives to attract foreign investors. Recently my husband and I have seen a lot of foreign investors purchasing real estate properties in Las Vegas,

Nevada and Miami, Florida. Many of these properties are purchased with cash.

What to look for when purchasing an international property?

Before purchasing an international vacation property, identify a country where you would like to visit often. Primarily it is your vacation home so it should be a location you would enjoy visiting often.

As with a vacation home in the United States, you will need to consider the cash flow analysis before purchasing an international vacation property. Consider the maintenance costs that come with owning a vacation home in that country and then look at typical rental potential of your international home.

Another factor to consider is how you are going to manage the property. Are there property managers in that country that you can trust and work with? This is not a time to act with emotion but first figure out all the logistics and then make the purchase. Research into the banking system of the country you are going to purchase in and any real estate related laws that you need to be aware of. It is better to work with international real estate firms such as "International Living" that could make the research easier for you. With the advancement in the internet, it is not difficult to research and find the right partners that you need to work with.

I personally would advise looking into this international option after you have had some experience in the real estate investment business. If this is the only option you are looking at, take your time to do enough research and then make a decision. My husband and I had visited some countries and decided not to invest in the properties available there.

Rule of Thumb : Basic advice for purchasing an international real estate property is to make personal visits to these places. Don't make a decision based on talking to someone on the phone or researching on the internet. International real estate properties should be handled with great deal of care and wisdom. When you visit the place, you not only look at the property itself but you also look at other logistics.

How are the roads maintained, and how easy is it to reach the resort? Would renters complaint about the upkeep of the resort or the access to it? What kind of demographics relate to the vacation home property? Are groceries easily available and is the food healthy? Are there any other health or demographic hazards one needs to be aware of before making a decision?

A very important factor for me personally was to look at the availability of medical help in and around the area. Although vacations are supposed to be fun, we do run into health problems every now and then and

you don't want to be stranded on an island with less
than appropriate medical help.

Example of cash flow calculation

Let's take a look at a typical property. If the purchase
price is $250,000 and assuming the investor pays 20
percent down, the loan is going to be for $200,000.
Let's assume that the loan is 15 year fixed with a
mortgage rate of 8 percent. Mortgage rates will vary
from country to country and are typically higher.

If the daily average rental is $125 and the investor is
able to rent it on average 20 days of the month, the
monthly rental income is $2500. Let's assume the
investor is going to hire a property manager for this
foreign investment which is more likely than not.

Monthly Rental income = $2500
Monthly Mortgage payment = $1911 (Principal + Interest)
Monthly property tax = 0 (Assuming no property tax in
foreign country)
Monthly HOA fee = $90 (Assuming lower HOA fee in
foreign country)
Monthly Property management fee = $200

Cash Flow = $2500 - $1911 - $90 - $200 = $299

In the above example, the investor is cash flow
positive despite paying the extra fee of property
management in the foreign country and a higher

mortgage rate. He may or may not be cash flow positive in all the months, depending on the tourism season. Some months may be fully rented out and some months may have very few rentals because those months are not in high tourism season. However, when averaged over the year, the investor should be at least cash flow even. Assuming he is able to rent it for the same duration throughout the year, his yearly cash flow will be $3588.

In order to avoid paying high mortgage rates in a foreign country, you could pay by cash. This is a decision you need to make as an investor and how it relates to your goals and budget. Again comparing cash flow numbers of an international vacation home to that of a vacation home in the United States would not be wise. The key is to always do the cash flow calculation ahead of time to understand your expenses and potential income situation. The cash flow calculation should align with your real estate investment goals.

6 FORECLOSURES AND SHORT SALES

For a real estate investor looking for a steady income on his rental property, acquiring a short sale or property via foreclosure was a lucrative yet not a feasible option until recently.

Foreclosure and short sales were terms we did not hear much about until recently. The reason was because a home owner typically used to make a 20 percent down payment when purchasing a real estate property. For a property to lose 20 percent of its value was not a common occurrence and hence foreclosures and short sales were not common.

About a decade back with changes in mortgage underwriting rules, loans were encouraged and given with zero down payment. The belief was that homes never lose value hence it is okay to give out loans with zero down payment. As house prices rose, homeowners re-financed to a higher mortgage with the new value and still owed almost 100 percent of the amount of the new value of the loan. What made the situation worse was that on top of not putting any down payment, homeowners took out variable rate loans, for a very low rate.

When house prices started to show signs of softening, people got alarmed looking at their high mortgage payments and lower house value. They could not refinance to a lower house value and their monthly mortgage payments were still quite high. This led to people panicking and defaulting on their loans and going to foreclosure. Foreclosed properties typically sell for a lower price than an equivalent regular sale.

Initially banks were not prepared to deal with this flood of short sales. However, this reality needs to be faced. Home Affordable Foreclosure Alternatives (HAFA) program has streamlined the process for those dealing with these situations.

Short sale is a process where a bank agrees to sell a property for an amount lower than the current loan on the house. If a home goes to foreclosure, it is typically more expensive for the bank, hence recently they have become more agreeable to the short sale process. A foreclosed home is sold free of any liens, just like a regular home. A short sale, however may have other hidden factors and typically takes much longer time to close, possibly three to six months.

Investors were afraid to touch foreclosures or short sales due to the length of time it took to complete the process of acquiring a distressed property. With HAFA program in place, the time duration and the process for acquiring a distressed property is more predictable. This then becomes a more lucrative option especially in those states where the difference in prices of non-distressed to distressed homes is larger.

What to look for when purchasing a foreclosed home?

Purchasing a foreclosed property or acquiring a property through short sale has the same factors associated with it as that for single family home. The only additional step is to make sure that the property has not been tampered with in any shape or form. In most cases short sales and foreclosures are sold "as is", which means the seller will not make any repairs to the house before selling. You need to factor in the cost to fix those issues in determining the offer price.

Some distressed home owners may attempt to destroy the home or cause trouble. Again, if you hire a good inspector, they can help you evaluate the property. An additional factor to consider with short sales, is that typically the home owner is still living in the property. You run the risk that they may damage the property after you have done the inspection but before you get possession. You need to factor in this possibility when dealing with short sales. You also need to remember that the time required to acquire a foreclosed or short sale is longer due to their process. It is also better to work with a real estate agent who has experience in handling distressed properties so he can help close things faster and smoother.

As usual, the number one thing to consider is the price of the property. You must determine whether the rental income of the area would be enough for you as an investor to be cash flow positive. Don't buy a property unless you are sure about being cash flow positive. The last thing you want to do is pay the mortgage from your own pocket.

You also need to look at the neighborhood, Is it safe, is it a growing market in terms of job and economy and companies? Would renters prefer staying in this area versus other areas of the city? Are the schools of this neighborhood good enough? Are there groceries stores and malls accessible from the rental property?

My husband and I didn't consider this option in our acquisition of single family homes but recently this option has become quite lucrative and many investors are seriously looking to acquire properties by this route.

Example of cash flow calculation

Lets say a single home property in pristine condition is going for $140k. However, a similar property is listed for $120k in foreclosure. You determine that it will take $5000 to fix the property. You are getting this property for less but have some risks since it is a foreclosure. Your cash flow numbers will work better on a monthly basis but you need to come up with the additional $5000 to fix the property since banks will typically give you loan on $120k. Lets assume, the investor pays 20 percent down payment. The loan is going to be for $96,000. Lets say, the loan is 15 year fixed with a mortgage rate of 4 percent

For rent calculation, let's assume we will get a round about 1 percent of a typical purchase price of $140,000 as monthly rental, for example, $1400 monthly rental in this case is a good solid number to shoot for.

Monthly Rental income = $1400
Monthly Mortgage payment = $710 (Principal + Interest)
Monthly HOA fees = $25
Monthly property tax = $115
Monthly insurance expense = $75

Cash Flow $= \$1400 - \$710 - \$25 - \$115 - \$75 = \$475$

In this example, the investor is making a good profit on the rental property. He purchased it for a good price as result of it being a foreclosed property and therefore his cost basis is low. If he is able to rent it out throughout the year, his yearly cash flow will be $5700. But recall, he had to spend $5000 to fix it, therefore he need not pay any taxes for the first couple of years to offset the cost of capital additions.

7 MORTGAGE

A mortgage is a loan on your real estate investment property. Since your property is used as security to ensure that you will repay the money, it is important to understand your options. If you are not going to pay cash for your real estate property, you will be taking loan from a bank.

Single family homes are easiest to get a mortgage on. You may have difficulty getting a mortgage for condominiums and international investments, so again you should check on it before you go too far into your planning. There are on line mortgage calculators you can use to calculate your monthly mortgage payments. http://www.mortgagecalculator.org/ is a good resource to utilize for your calculations.

Before you make an offer on a real estate property you should be pre-approved for the loan. This not only provides you peace of mind but also makes your offer better. In fact in most cases the seller would like to see such a pre-approval before they even look at your offer.

In terms of loan amount, you have three choices. A conventional mortgage loan does not exceed 80 percent of the home price. A high-ratio mortgage is a loan that is above 80 percent but below 95 percent of the purchase price of the house. High-ratio mortgages must be insured against loss, and the insurance premium is added to the loan price. Another option for financing up to 95 percent of purchase price is to get two mortgage loans. The first mortgage lender has the right to the property in case of default. The second lender therefore charges a high interest rate due to higher risk.

Let's look at the mechanics of a mortgage. In a fixed-term mortgage, the interest rate is fixed for the duration of the loan. In an adjustable rate mortgage (A.R.M.) there is a lot of flexibility where rates can be adjusted on a monthly basis. There is also the option of multiple term mortgages where the loan is customized such as adjustable for three years and fixed for ten years. You can split the entire duration of loan into five parts. This is for the more hands-on people who keep an eye on interest rate fluctuations. Another option is the 6-month convertible mortgage when interest rates are going down. You can have the option of six months at a fixed payment and then have the advantage of converting the loan to a longer–term, less-risky loan. Considering how low mortgage rates are in today's market, a Fixed-Term mortgage is the best way to go about getting your real estate property financed.

You need to also ensure that the mortgage you are taking has no pre-payment penalty. When you take the loan, you may take it for thirty year fixed period but later decide to pay it off in lets say twenty years. In such a scenario, you do not want to pay any pre-payment penalty.

Rule of Thumb : Do not listen to those who tell you to put zero down payment. This may seem like a lucrative option but you know there is no such thing as a free lunch. In this case, you pay the price by having a higher mortgage rate. Always aim to have a 20 percent down payment in cash to get the best deal possible on your mortgage rate.

My advice is to prepare to put at-least 20 percent down and get pre-approved for fifteen year or thirty year fixed mortgage. Remember that fifteen year loan has a higher monthly payment (since a much higher amount is going towards the principal) than a thirty year fixed loan. Run the numbers to make sure you are comfortable with the fifteen year loan. If not then go for thirty year fixed. You can always make additional principal payments during the life of the loan.

Why make 20 percent down payment

You may ask, why should I put 20 percent down, shouldn't I leverage with a smaller down payment? The answer is yes you can do that and it may be an option if you do not have enough cash for 20 percent down payment. Although I would advise you not to invest in real estate if you do not currently have 20 percent down payment and wait till you have it. You get the best rate with lowest costs when you put at-least 20 percent down payment and have good credit scores.

When my husband and I started investing in real estate we had 20 percent down payment, but our mortgage broker at that time advised us that since we were getting the property at a good price based upon appraised value, we should only pay 10 percent down. Since our down payment was less than 20 percent, we had to make PMI (private mortgage insurance) payments, which was about $100 per month. He said that after six months the PMI could be waived by the mortgage company since our loan to value would be less than 80 percent. Since we were just starting off, we took the advice and put 10 percent down. Six months later when we called our broker, he said to call the mortgage company directly to have the PMI waived. We called the mortgage company and they told us they would only waive the PMI if our loan to value was 65 percent or less and that we would need to get an appraisal done (which costs about $400). We knew that we were not yet at 65 percent and luckily since interest rates had come down we refinanced with additional down payment to have 20 percent down and no PMI. You must have guessed it -- we did not use our original mortgage broker to do our refinancing.

Mortgage rate for investment properties

You need to be aware that mortgage rates for your primary home and your investment properties are going to be different. The mortgage rates for investment properties are generally higher than those of your primary home. These rates are going to be about three-quarter percent higher than those of your primary homes. In some cases where you could qualify a real estate property as your second home, you could get a lower mortgage rate but for all other properties, the mortgage rates are going to be higher. There are very strict guidelines on what qualifies as second home so before you decide to do that, be extra cautious. You need to be able to show that you are living in that home for a certain length of time each year. Unless, you truly are doing that, it is safer to qualify it as an investment property.

8 PROPERTY MANAGEMENT

Now that we have looked at several different options for acquiring a rental property, lets also look at the next step in the process. You have done the hard work of picking a good property and gone through the entire process of financing and closing the deal on the property. Now comes the exciting time to find a potential renter for the property or making it available for vacation home depending on which type of property you have purchased.

This is a very exciting yet responsible part of the process. You need to do due diligence in picking up reliable, long-term renters with whom you can easily work. You can handle the entire process yourself or you can hire a property manager. It all depends on whether you are ready to do the work and if so, are you living in the same place where your rental property is.

It is certainly advisable to buy a rental property near where you reside but it is not always possible. If you are new to the process, it may be better to hire a property manager, at least for your first rental property. Once you have learned the process, you could do it yourself.

Property management for single family homes

There are different aspects of property management ranging from arranging an open house to renting the property to discussing lease agreement with your renters to maintenance of the property once it is rented. The process repeats itself once a renter leaves or his lease expires.

During this entire process, one important thing to keep in mind is that customer or renter is the king, treat him like one! Listen to their needs, desires and be understanding. For example, if there is a leak in the house reported by your renter, get to it right away. Put yourself in their shoes and do the right thing. As in any other business if the customer is treated right they will be loyal to you.

If you are working with a property manager they will do the advertising, get rental applications and qualify the tenants. They should work closely with you throughout this process and provide you with regular updates. At the same time you should remember they are working on many different properties simultaneously so you should be proactively interacting with them from a review perspective.

On the other hand, if you are managing the property yourself, you have lot more flexibility as well as responsibility. You can advertise your property in Craigslist and other internet sites like hotpads.com etc. These days most of the business is done online so that is where you should advertise. It is very important to be truthful in your advertisement and not oversell the property. Doing so will only hurt you. You can get the renter to come see the property but you won't get them to rent it. It is also about your reputation. Much like any other business, building a solid reputation goes a long way. Say it like it is, show it like it is. Tell your renters what they are in for and they will be loyal to you. If you price your home competently you should be able to get interest in your property soon. Make the house ready as if you are going to sell it prior to showing it to prospective tenants. You want your house to look the best possible when you show it.

How to set the monthly rent?

Setting monthly rent is the most important aspect when putting your home for rent on the market. If you set it too high it may take a long time to rent your property whereas if you set it too low you are leaving money on the table. You should do rental comparison analysis in the market for similar homes. My recommendation is to price your home slightly below the market if the numbers still work for you in your cash flow analysis. The main reason is that if your house takes one month to rent (at the higher price) but can get rented right away at a slightly lower price, you will still come out ahead over the course of the lease.

Ask any prospective tenant to fill out an application, you need an application from each adult who is going to live in the house. You can also ask them to provide you with their credit report (anyone can get a free credit report for themselves online). You can also run their credit report with permission from them.

How to qualify a tenant

Once you have the prospective tenant's application and the credit report, there are further steps to evaluate their application. You should also meet with the tenants and the family. Sometimes a face to face meeting and interaction reveals more information. Let's look at some of the checks you need to perform before renting your home.

- **Credit check** – You should check the credit report for their credit score, outstanding debt etc. They may not have the best credit scores but you should look for any evictions in their past. If they have had evictions, that is a red flag and you should ask them for an explanation. A lot of people have fallen on hard times and have had foreclosures or short sales of their primary residence. You should evaluate this on a case by case basis, although this in itself may not be a big deal if other criterion work out.

- **Employment Check** – The tenant should be currently employed and be making enough money to be able to pay the rent and other expenses. Ask for their previous two pay check vouchers and verify with the employer.

- **Criminal Check** – You can optionally do their criminal background check as well.

Once you are comfortable with the above mentioned checks and if both parties agree you enter into a lease agreement. Standard lease for single family homes is for a year but you can sign a longer term lease if you wish. I do not recommend offering a lease less than one year. Typically you will also include a security deposit amount, which is approximately one month's rent. The security deposit cannot be used as rent but will be returned back to tenant, less any cleaning or damage charges, when they vacate the property at the end of their lease.

Property management for vacation homes

Renting vacation homes require a more hands on approach. Depending upon the area, your renters may be looking for a place to rent for a short duration, somewhere from a weekend to a few weeks.

Advertising – vrbo.com and homeaway.com are the two most prominent websites where you could advertise your vacation home. I do not recommend advertising on craigslist for vacation homes. My husband and I tried it but only got people who were lowballers and did not result in any success. Make sure you have some good quality pictures of the vacation home that show your property as well as the surroundings. You should also highlight the amenities that will interest a potential traveler and make them want to stay in your property. Highlight keywords in the heading of your vacation rental advertisement. You can certainly look for advertisements in similar areas to get ideas.

Pricing – Just like single family home rentals, pricing is key for your vacation home as well. You are competing with hotels as well as other vacation rentals in the area. Granted, in most cases a vacation rental property is better and has more amenities than a hotel, so you can command a slightly higher rate. You have to be somewhat flexible in your pricing specially if you have a vacancy for the dates in the next three to four weeks and you suspect you may not be able to fill the property. Of course you can hold your rates if the dates in question are months in the future. Furthermore you should provide discounted rate for longer rental. For example, you may charge $120 a night for the weekend nights, and $600 for a full week. You may charge $1100 for two weeks but $1900 for a full month. As you can see the longer the renter stays, the higher the discount that you would offer to them. Hotels typically do not follow this pricing model and hence vacation homes are a good option for people who rent for slightly longer term.

Also try to find longer term renters if your dates are in the future. Longer term for vacation rentals means one week or more. This will help you minimize the vacancies and will have less wear and tear on your property. Of course the goal is to keep your property

100 percent occupied so as the dates gets closer be flexible on shorter term rentals as well. Typically it makes sense for you as well as your renter if they are renting for three or more days. Anything less you will not be able to make much money if you offer them a price advantage. Sometimes it is better to leave the property empty than to rent to someone for one or two nights at a small revenue.

You want people who are not necessarily looking for the cheapest rental, but someone who is looking for a fair price and will respect and appreciate your property. Of course everyone wants a deal but if your renter appreciates the amenities of your property and wants to enjoy the experience, they should be willing to pay a fair price.

You should also consider how many people will be staying there. It makes a big difference whether there are only one or two people or is it closer to four people crowding into a one bedroom condominium. Many hotels don't care if it is four people but you should charge extra per person if such is the case. More people in your property means more wear and tear so you should adjust your pricing accordingly.

Communication – Timely communication with potential renters who respond to your vacation rental advertisement is extremely important. You should respond to them within 24 hours. Also be very clear and explicit about what is included in your price and provide a complete breakdown of the costs. Keep a template for communication and customize it in your response as needed. This will reduce the back and forth communication and the potential renter will appreciate all the information they can get from you in the beginning.

Property manager and cleaners – Unless you live in the area you would need a property manager and a cleaning service company. Property managers typically charge 15 – 25 percent of collected rent for vacation homes, therefore if you can manage without them, you will have a better cash flow. Even if you utilize a property management company, I recommend you still do the additional advertizing and marketing of your property. Keep in communication with your property manager to avoid any double bookings and if possible use a common calendar for bookings. If your vacation home is in a resort, you may be able to hire a cleaning company and use the resort service to give and collect keys. You can do the rest of the communication, collect rents etc. directly from the renters. This way you can avoid having to hire property managers. As far as cleaning goes, In most cases vacation homes do not include daily cleanings. You need to be upfront with your renters on what your policy is in regards to cleaning and how often you would offer it.

9 TAXES ON REAL ESTATE INVESTMENT

Much like other investment options, real estate investing has tax implications as well. You need to understand these implications before filing your taxes. You don't need to know everything before you get in the market but definitely before you file taxes. Knowing all the details is very necessary so that you don't overpay or underpay taxes. You don't want to be audited for the wrong reasons by IRS. If you don't feel confident, you can either consult or hire a CPA to maintain your annual taxes. Some investors consult a CPA for at least the first year and then once they feel more comfortable, they start doing their taxes themselves. Of course with the help of software like TurboTax, it is not difficult to file your own taxes because the software automates the process and avoids mistakes. But one thing the software doesn't do is explain the high level concepts associated with filing real estate related taxes. It is very important to understand the overall scheme of things before you file your first taxes related to your real estate investment.

Different categories of taxable income

At a very high level, what you need to know is that IRS qualifies taxable income in three different categories. The very first category is your earned income i.e. your paycheck and you pay your taxes based on which bracket your income falls into. The second category is your investment income which is basically the income you earn from stocks, mutual funds, bonds, ETFs etc. The third category is called passive income. Real estate income falls into this third category. The difference between investment income and passive income is that you can deduct losses (up to $3000) on investment income from your earned income, however, you cannot deduct losses from passive income from your earned income. Any losses you incur in real estate investment stays in that category. You can however carry your real estate investment losses to next year taxation. This is an essential difference that you need to know upfront before getting into the real estate investment business.

Filing of real estate taxes

You do file a separate form for your passive income related to real estate investment and it is called Schedule E. You will need to fill in details of your investment property, mortgage payments and other expenses related to the real estate property. Needless to say, you need to be organized throughout the year and keep this data current preferable in an accounting software such as Quickbooks.

Quickbooks makes it easier to organize your data in the right buckets and if you keep it updated throughout the year, it makes tax time a piece of cake. In order to utilize QuickBooks fully, it would be better to take a short course on accounting principles as well as study the QuickBooks tutorial well before you input your data. Your data needs to be organized in the right manner so it is readily available at taxation time. Lets look at different pieces of the puzzle for Schedule E.

Depreciation of property

IRS has set guidelines for depreciation of real estate property for the purposes of taxation. Each real estate property is depreciated over a period of 27.5 years depending on the cost of the structure. Land price is not part of the depreciation. When you purchase a real estate property you need to figure out this amount for tax purposes. There are couple of ways to figure this out, either you go by county appraisal of your property. Or you calculate it from your private appraisal whichever is higher. You want to pick the higher price since this is going to reduce your taxes. You basically reduce the yearly depreciation amount from your rental income. Technically even though you may be cash flow positive on your real estate property, after you deduct the depreciation amount, you may not have to pay taxes at all.

How to calculate

Depreciation amount = Depreciation Basis/ Useful Life

Useful life of a residential property is 27.5 years

Amortization

Another concept you need to be aware of as part of real estate tax filing is amortization. This is similar to depreciation but applies to the costs you incurred when applying for a loan for your real estate property. The cost is then divided over the period of the loan and each year you deduct this amount from your real estate income.

How to calculate real estate taxable income

When you are filing taxes on real estate properties, one thing to keep in mind is that you don't include the principal amount of the mortgage in your expenses. When you are making your mortgage payment, you are paying some amount towards the principal and some as interest. What you subtract from rental income is only the interest portion of your mortgage payment. The formula for figuring out taxable income is as follows :

Annual Rental Income

less Annual Expenses (Mortgage interest payment, property tax, insurance, any other expense)

less Depreciation amount

less Amortization

= Taxable income

Like Exchange

I recommend buying property and holding it for a long time. Over time you own the property free and clear and use the income to supplement your retirement. You may also sell your property when your kids are ready to go to college to pay their tuition. If you do want to sell a property, you need to pay taxes on the capital gains and this pretty much washes out the depreciation amount that you had been filing in your taxes. However, there is a way to avoid paying this tax if you purchase another property for a higher price than the property that you are selling. It is called 1031 exchange or Like Exchange. There are certain guidelines for qualifying a property as a like exchange, one of course is the price -- the other is that it be a similar type of property in a similar neighborhood. This is common practice to defer paying taxes on your property sale indefinitely.

10 TIPS FOR SUCCESS

As you can tell by now, investing in real estate is not an easy task. It requires a great amount of discipline and understanding of details and concepts to make the right decisions at the right time. It certainly is an involved process. Let me share some useful tips to help you succeed in your real estate investment venture.

- ⚐ Assemble a trustworthy team ahead of time before purchasing your property. Things will move fast and you will need your team's help throughout the process.

- ⚐ When deciding to purchase a real estate property, try to strike a good balance between current cash flow and future appreciation. Don't buy something which has good cash flow but no potential for appreciation.

- ⚐ Do some research to check out the neighborhood in which you are buying the property. Buy in established areas with good schools and a growing population as well as job market. Although your goal is to be more cash flow positive, you also need to consider other aspects of this business. If you buy a less expensive property in a not-so-good neighborhood, you may have more cash flow. However, you may be dealing with not-so-good renters. Good renters usually want to live in a good neighborhood. Considering the ease of business aspects is also of equal importance. Try to strike a balance between cash flow and ease of business.

⅄ Take your time to understand the market and the properties you are looking at. It is often easier to buy a property than to sell it, therefore you need to put some thought into the purchase. When you are ready to sell a property, it takes anywhere from eight to ten percent of the cost, which covers six percent agent commission and other expenses. The last thing you want is to sell a property because you bought something you don't want.

⅄ Do research into data pertaining to the market where you are buying the property. Look at the statistics but don't fall prey to "analysis paralysis". If you spend too much time thinking and analyzing it will make the decision making process much harder. Use intuition combined with concrete data to make sound decisions for the property you want to purchase.

⅄ When you are ready to make your purchase, have at least 20 percent down payment in cash. Also, get an approval for the loan amount from the mortgage broker or bank. Don't listen to people who will tell you to put zero down payment, it will not work for your business. It is only going to complicate things in the long run. Try to go for a fifteen year or thirty year fixed mortgage with 20 percent down payment on your loan to get the best interest rate possible.

⅄ When possible, try handling the different tasks involved yourself, rather than going through a middle person. You will make more profits that way and you will be more cash flow positive. If you are working with partners, try to figure out their motivation. Ask questions and build trust. Try to build long term partnership and sharing of profit model as much as possible.

⋏ Always put your customer i.e. renter ahead of yourself and you will be ahead in the long term. Much like any other business, customer satisfaction is a big deal in this business as well. Listening to renter's needs and complaints and responding timely is in the interest of the investor.

⋏ Build relationships with trustworthy partners such as your real estate agent, your mortgage broker and your property manager if you have one. It is very important to have trust in these partners for the success of your business.

⋏ If you are renting out a single family home, it is a good idea to find a reliable and trustworthy handyman who can serve your needs with a quick turnaround. For example, if your renters complaint about a leak in the house, you would want to get it fixed as soon as possible.

⋏ Don't be late in paying your HOA fees. It might cause discomfort to your renters, a situation you want to avoid. Keep reminders in your calendar to avoid such a situation. Nevertheless if such a situation occurs, don't panic and handle it gracefully.

⋏ Keep records of all your transactions, rental income, expenses, anything related to real estate in a good accounting software such as QuickBooks. It will come in handy at taxation time. You want to be prepared with all the data when you file taxes.

APPENDIX

As a first time investor, you may feel overwhelmed with the different tasks involved in acquiring, renting and maintaining a real estate property.

Here are a few checklists that you can use throughout the process.

Checklist for finding the right property

- ⚔ Work with a reliable real estate agent who specializes in investment properties.

- ⚔ First thing first, check to determine if at the current purchase price, you will be cash flow positive or not.

- ⚔ In order to calculate your cash flow, make use of online mortgage calculators such as http://www.mortgagecalculator.org/

- ⚔ Consider the location. Is the property in a good neighborhood? Is there a decent school in the neighborhood? Would the property attract good-quality renters?

- ⅄ What is the upward price potential for the property you are interested in?

Checklist for mortgage

- ⅄ Work with a trustworthy mortgage agent who will get you the best rate and close in time.

- ⅄ Aim for 20 percent down payment on your property. You will get the best interest rate.

- ⅄ Consider a 15 year or 30 year fixed loan whichever works best for your cash flow calculation.

Checklist for renting your property

- ⅄ Charge a minimal rental application fee ($25) to attract only serious renters.

- ⅄ Ask for credit history and employment information from your potential renters.

- ⅄ Ensure all corner cases are documented in the lease agreement as it relates to late payment or any damages in the property or pet policy.

- Utilize the Craigslist website to place your advertisement for renting your single family home.

- For vacation homes, VRBO (Vacation Rental By Owner) is an excellent resource that will help you market your vacation home as well as get potential renters. You can also research similar properties that are currently on this site to determine your rent price.

- Be honest in your advertisement of your property.

- Ask for reviews from your renters and show reviews on your VRBO rental property website. A lot of potential renters rely heavily on the reviews when determining whether they want to rent from you.

Internet Resources

Following are some internet websites that can be useful for doing your research.

- zillow.com

- bankrate.com

- redfin.com

- mortgagecalculator.org

As an investor you ought to be familiar with certain forms that you will need to fill out throughout the process. Some forms will be filled by you as an investor and other ones will be agreement with the renters. I have included a list of resources where you can get these forms in this appendix.

⅄ For Lease agreements

- www.ezlandlordforms.com
- www.mrlandlord.com

⅄ For Schedule E

- www.irs.gov/pub/irs-pdf/f1040se.pdf

ABOUT THE AUTHOR

Aditi Chopra is a motivating leader, process consultant and a creative writer. She utilizes her experience in software engineering, people management and communication strategies to help create value for organizations. She has authored books on Business Process Management and Leadership skills. Her knowledge of real estate investment comes from her personal experience and not as a real estate professional.

www.ingramcontent.com/pod-product-compliance
Lightning Source LLC
Chambersburg PA
CBHW071624170526
45166CB00003B/1181